Jason Irwin

STOCK MARKET GUIDE FOR BEGINNERS 2021/2022:

INVESTMENT OPPORTUNITIES

Learn how to invest in options and how to trade in the stock market with the best investment opportunities

Table of Contents

INTRODUCTION 1

CHAPTER 1   CREATE A PASSIVE INCOME WITH DIVIDEND STOCKS 4

ACTIVE INCOME... 7

CHAPTER 2   OPTIONS 101: THE LOWEST RISKS INVESTMENT 8

CHAPTER 3   PRICE-EARNINGS RATIO (P/E) AND VALUE INVESTING..........12

WHAT IS THE PRICE-EARNINGS RATIO? 12

WHAT IS THE VALUE INVESTING METHODOLOGY?.................................. 13

CHAPTER 4   MAKE MONEY WITH GROWTH STOCKS AND IPOS 17

IGNORE THE HIGH P/E 17

UNDERSTANDING IPOS.. 22

CHAPTER 5   ADVANCED ANALYSIS 28

FUNDAMENTAL ANALYSIS 29

TECHNICAL ANALYSIS 36

CHAPTER 6   MAKE MONEY WITH IPOS 41

TAKE FULL ADVANTAGE OF THE TIME... 41

PRACTICE INVESTING REGULARLY 43

MAINTAIN A PORTFOLIO THAT IS DIVERSE 44

TAKE THE HELP OF SOME PROFESSIONAL.. 45

HOW TO SUCCEED IN THE STOCK MARKET? 45

CHAPTER 7   EXCHANGE-TRADED FUNDS 47

ETFS OFFER AUTOMATIC DIVERSITY 48

THE MAIN COMPANIES OFFERING ETFS.. 49

ETFs and Dividends 55

ETFs Make It Easy 55

CHAPTER 8   FUTURES 57

Pros of Futures Trading.. 59

Cons of Futures Trading 60

Speculation of Futures.. 62

Futures Hedging... 64

Futures Regulation 65

Example of Futures Trading 65

CHAPTER 9   MUTUAL FUNDS..67

Types of Mutual Funds 70

How to Invest in Mutual Funds 74

The Benefits of Investing in Mutual Funds............................ 79

CHAPTER 10   HOW TO MINIMIZE LOSSES AND MAXIMIZE GAINS WITH STOCKS?   80

Securities Market Manipulation—How to Protect Yourself 83

Leave Strategies That Lock in Profits and/or Minimize Losses 85

How Much Threat Are We Willing to Take? 88

Where Do We Desire to Obtain Out? 89

CHAPTER 11   FACTORS AFFECTING THE STOCK MARKET.......................90

Economy 90

Political Events... 91

Media.. 91

Supply and Demand 91

Natural Disasters 92

INVESTORS THEMSELVES... 93

MARKETING HYPE 93

WORLD EVENTS.. 94

NEWS 94

DEFLATION 95

CHAPTER 12   MAJOR STOCK EXCHANGES 102

THE FOUR MAJOR EXCHANGES... 102

OTHER POPULAR AND MAJOR EXCHANGES 106

STOCK MARKET PERFORMANCE AND INDEXES 107

CONCLUSION 110

INTRODUCTION

Trading on the stock market requires a bit of courage. With millions of shares of stock trading back and forth across the exchange, you'll soon learn that you have to be quick at getting a clear understanding of the ebbs and flows of the market if you have any hope of surviving.

One of the first things to know is that the exchange is more than just a platform where you can buy and sell at will. It is also the agent that tracks each stock's supply and demand and therefore, sets the price of each stock.

But buying and selling stocks is not as simple as going into the supermarket and picking your shares up off the shelf. You have to understand exactly what you're buying, how to see its value, and how to analyze it properly so that you know if you're getting a good deal or not.

Most people understand that when you buy a stock, you are purchasing a percentage of the business, however, that is as far as their understanding goes. Many may also understand when they hear terms like the market is up or down that they are referring to the price, but for others, this may not be all that clear. So, let's return to the basics and get a clearer understanding of what all of these phrases and terms actually mean.

Generally speaking, when you hear phrases like "the market is up" or "the market is down," these are not referring to individual stocks, but instead are referring to market indexes. A market index is a group of stocks from the same industry sector. An example of some familiar market indexes could be technology, retail, energy, or biotechnology.

Some of the most common indexes you've probably already heard are the Standard & Poor's 50, the Dow Jones Industrial Average, or the NASDAQ composite. These are often used as a tool to get a picture of the overall market conditions and can serve as a benchmark for investors to evaluate the condition of their stock portfolios. If you are fascinated by investing in a particular index but don't have the time to research each company in a particular sector, you could invest in an index simply by purchasing a share in an index fund or an Exchange-Traded Fund (ETF).

A good stock analysis is a key factor in investing success. It is the most dependable means of finding those gems of a stock that can produce potentially profitable returns. The fundamentals we just went through can be considered different forms of technical analysis. These permit you to get a closer look at the supply and demands of any stock within the market. Investors who rely on this form of analysis rely heavily on a stock's historical performance and use it as a predictor of what they could reasonably expect in the future. With technical analysis, there is a great deal of emphasis on trends, charts, and patterns.

There is, however, another method of analyzing stocks that is very different from performing a technical analysis. Fundamental analysis is a very broad area that can be difficult for newbies to the market to master. It requires the investor to be familiar with a number of different variables including financial statements, regulatory findings, and a number of different valuation techniques.

CHAPTER 1   CREATE A PASSIVE INCOME WITH DIVIDEND STOCKS

All you really need to do is open your eyes and see what others in the community are doing.

Dividend stocks might not be for everyone, but they can produce a passive income at a rate higher than 1%. The best part is that it's practical, friendly to beginners, and cheap to get started with.

The secret to this strategy is a stock index fund coupled with the right investment strategy. Dividend Funds will increase your returns faster than actively managed funds. If you don't know much about dividend funds, there are two that I personally use and recommend. The first is the Vanguard Dividend Appreciation Fund ETF (VIG). It's constructed using various companies that pay a steady dividend and are globally diversified. The second is the Fidelity Dividend Advantage Fund (FDV). This fund uses large-cap stocks that pay a dividend and will increase your rate of return in the future. If you choose to invest in any form of passive dividend stocks, be sure to pick ones that are globally diversified or concentrated in a specific country's market capitalization.

Dividend Stocks—Your guide to Passive Income

As I was saying, I don't think there's anything taboo about investing in dividend stocks. Everyone wants passive income and it's a great way to earn it. Even if you tell people that you're only going to own stocks that pay a dividend, you'll be hard-pressed to find someone who doesn't want that kind of stability in their portfolio. The question is, how can investors get started? What are the best stocks to invest in for dividend yields?

The best answer I can give is that there's no clear answer to these questions. Dividend investing is a risk, but it's one that will pay off handsomely. High dividend stocks can give you a passive income at rates higher than 1%. There are many ways to invest in dividend stocks. You can purchase them directly from the stock market or use stock exchanges like trade or Scottrade. If you're a person who wants to diversify, you can buy an index fund or Exchange-traded fund (ETF) that specializes in dividends and interest-rate environments.

With the current market and economy, finding an investment that is safe and rewards you with even more is tough to find. Dividend stocks are a great thing to invest in because they give back some of their earnings every quarter. They have been proven to provide a stable income but still provide growth.

This is why dividend stocks have seen a sharp increase in popularity as interest rates start creeping up again. Dividend stocks are great long-term investments because you aren't at risk of losing all of your money if you sell them down the road.

Active Income

Investing for the sole purpose of making money is a bad idea. You need to want to make money in order to make it happen. If you only want to make money passively by investing in dividend stocks, then that is fine but that's not the only way. You can also have an active income and be your own boss.

Having an active income is a great way to generate money and not have to worry about the market or economy. Many people quit their day job because they are generating enough online. This is something you should look into if you want to take control of your financial future.

CHAPTER 2 OPTIONS 101: THE LOWEST RISKS INVESTMENT

If you're looking for maximum upside potential and lower risk than with any other type of investment, then options might be your best bet. That's right...

- Investing in options is not only a low-risk way to make money but it also offers higher returns on invested capital.

- Options provide a greater ability to create leverage by owning tiny amounts of stock or shares on top of thousands of dollars of underlying investments.

- Options come with slightly less risk than investing directly in the underlying stock.

- Because options often have a far longer life than their underlying stocks, they can offer longer time horizons for investors who are interested in participating in a trend.

Options trade on major exchanges for two main reasons:

1. It is often easier to find buyers of options than it is to find sellers.

2. Using options requires less capital investment than buying/selling securities outright.

According to the IRS, there are two types of investors, one sets gains while another sets income. If you want a higher return on your investment but you don't want to risk as much then you should be investing in options. Using options trading will help you get the maximum amount of capital that you can earn with the least risk possible.

Options trading can be done by anyone using some basic information about how they work and understanding of the [strike price quote] and [expiration] date.

Options are a complicated, yet powerful financial tool. They allow you to invest in something that is not currently available (i.e. stocks). However, the downside of options trading is risk and the option premium does not decrease as time progresses.

Even if you are willing to take on this risk, there are benefits of using options to make investments that might be troublesome or too complicated when they're done with stocks.

You Can Buy or Sell More Than One Type at Once

When someone buys a stock, they are buying a share of the entire company. If you buy one stock, that's it, you own the stock. On the other hand, if someone buys a call option from you (as long as the value is greater than zero), then they're paying to be guaranteed a profit of 100% on any future trade. With options, the same person can profit from any number of investment opportunities at once.

Options Are a Contract That You Make with the Seller

When you buy shares in a company it's because you believe that the future will be much better than today, so it costs less now to invest. However, with options, you're forfeiting this ability to time-value of money and are instead gambling that the stock will go up. You've also forfeited your ability to manage risk in the market as well since you are trusting someone else to determine when and if they will exercise their option for your benefit or not. On the other hand, if you sell (write) an option then you are guaranteeing to the buyer that they will receive a specific payoff in the future. This allows them to manage their risk as well as manage benefit rewards.

Since options are contracts that payoffs depend on, anyone trading them is a speculator (unless of course, they have knowledge of what the actual payoff will be for a particular contract). Traders speculate on expected returns from option premiums.

Options are nifty little financial instruments that peek at your investing appetite. They don't offer the same level of protection as things like stocks or bonds, but they offer some benefits that other investments just can't provide, and they're a great way to diversify your portfolio.

CHAPTER 3   PRICE-EARNINGS RATIO (P/E) AND VALUE INVESTING

What Is the Price-Earnings Ratio?

The price-to-earnings ratio, or P/E ratio, is a valuation metric that compares a company's share price to its per-share earnings.

Simply put, this P/E figure tells investors how much they are paying for each dollar of earnings. This metric should be used in conjunction with other metrics to make an informed investment decision.

What Is the Value Investing Methodology?

Value investing is a strategy that looks for companies with high growth rates and very low price-to-earnings multiples and sells them at a below-market price.

In essence, value investing is the practice of focusing on quality and future growth over profitability in order to invest in companies with strong prospects for long-term growth.

For example: Company X is trading at $100 per share and has earnings of $25 per share. This means the company is trading at a P/E multiple of 4:1, or 4 dollars for every $1 in earnings.

Company Y has earnings of $10 per share and is trading at a P/E multiple of 5:1, or 5 dollars for every $1 in earnings. Company Y has a higher/lower P/E ratio than Company X.

In most cases, this implies that Company Y is selling at a lower price than Company X. This means that investors can buy shares of Company Y for less per share than the same amount of cash.

Value investing is made more difficult for the investor when the current share price is below the company's intrinsic value, meaning it is selling for less than what it would cost to produce it (the "opportunity cost" of its assets).

Intrinsic value is a hypothetical number that incorporates all of the fundamentals of a company and estimates how much it would cost to replace the company with one of comparable quality.

These fundamentals include things like debt loads, growth prospects, profitability, and so on. Whenever a stock price falls below its intrinsic value, an opportunity for investors presents itself. The investor can buy shares and then wait for them to appreciate until they reach their intrinsic value.

Investors who practice value investing are playing the waiting game. Their strategy is simple: they buy shares of a stock that is selling for less than its intrinsic value and wait for the price to catch up to its true worth. When the price falls below the company's intrinsic value, it is considered "undervalued," and investors buy it in hopes that selling the company for its fair market value will net them a profit.

The goal of the value investor is to buy as many shares as possible below this intrinsic value. If the company gets sold for its intrinsic value, the investor pockets a profit. If it does not sell for its intrinsic value, the investor continues to hold their shares and wait—or may try to sell if they believe that it is undervalued.

Value investors make their money on the margins. They add up all of these little gains and losses and attempt to make a profit from them over time.

The Value Investing Methodology begins at the very beginning, with the company's valuation.

The first step is to look at the current stock price compared to its historical price (the "value metric"). Once they have a value metric, then it is time to determine the company's intrinsic value.

Value investors have to look at a number of metrics, including the price-to-earnings ratio, debt load (the amount of debt a company is carrying), and the growth prospects for the company. They also compare their knowledge of the company to that which can be found in readily available information, like public records. The price they come up with is heavily dependent on the amount of risk they believe they are taking with their investment. Value investors strive to find companies that are undervalued. They conduct a re-valuation of the company. If they believe the company is undervalued, they buy shares of the stock in hopes that it will eventually reach its intrinsic value. If it never reaches the intrinsic value, they sell their shares and pocket their profits. If it does reach that intrinsic value, then they can sell their shares for a profit and walk away with a better return on their investment than if they had invested in a different type of investment (i.e. bonds, mutual funds, etc.).

While value investing may be tempting in the short term, it is not a strategy that is likely to generate a profit in the long term.

CHAPTER 4 MAKE MONEY WITH GROWTH STOCKS AND IPOS

A growth stock is simply the stock of any company that is expected to grow its revenues or earnings rapidly. Here's the first rule for trading growth stocks:

Ignore the High P/E

Great companies that are rapidly growing will always trade at high P/Es. They might not even have any earnings. They might be losing a lot of money as they grow their market share, like Uber. They might also grow their market share for many years before they turn on the profit spigot. That's what Facebook did. It raised the social network for many years, before finally turning on advertising.

Value investors will always tell you to stay away from companies with high P/Es or companies that are losing money. But if you do that, you will miss some of the greatest stock runs of all time. Microsoft, Starbucks, Home Depot, and Amazon all traded at very high P/Es for many years. Amazon still does. But these stocks have gone on to make their holders very rich.

Companies with high P/Es are pricing in high growth in future earnings. If the growth is slowing or that those earnings may never appear, the market will trash the stock. That's why we always trade growth stocks with a clear stop loss.

If you are Warren Buffett investing in a mature company, the P/E does matter. If you are holding a growth stock for a few weeks or even months, nothing could matter less than the P/E.

Let me explain how to trade growth stocks. I like to buy growth stocks that are hitting new 52-week highs, or even all-time new highs. This may seem counter-intuitive to some. Isn't it risky to purchase a stock that is at all-time new highs? Doesn't that mean that it has further to fall?

If you study the highest growth stocks of the past, you will notice that they spend a lot of time trading at all-time new highs. This makes sense simply because any stock that goes up a lot must spend a lot of time trading at new highs.

There is, in fact, something wonderful and magical about a stock at an all-time high: Every single holder of the stock has a profit.

By contrast, when a stock has crashed or is continuously hitting new 52-week lows, many investors and traders have been left holding the bag. If the stock then tries to rally, these investors will be happy to get out by selling their shares at their break-even price. This provides constant downward pressure, and thus makes it more difficult for the stock to bounce back.

At a new all-time high, everyone who owns the stock has a profit. All the losers are gone and have already exited at a loss or their break-even price. At new highs, there are only happy traders and investors left. Well, except for one group of traders that no one feels sympathy very much for the short-sellers. These are traders who have shorted the stock (probably because "it has such a high P/E") and are betting that it will go down. At a new all-time high, everyone who has shorted the stock previously now has a losing trade on their hands. They are sweating bullets.

And there's only one thing that they can do to stem their losses: They must "cover" their shorts by buying back the stock. This buying only adds more fuel to the fire, driving the stock higher, and forcing out more short sellers.

Meanwhile, a stock that has recently moved up a lot begins to be featured on CNBC and explained by online commentators. This publicity brings in a new wave of buyers, who continue to drive the stock higher and make it hit even more new all-time highs.

The next step is to look at a daily chart of each stock. I want to make sure that the stock is trading above its 50-day moving average; and that the 50-day moving average is above the 200-day moving average.

Never buy a growth stock if the stock is trading below its 200-day moving average, or if the 50-day moving average is trading below the 200-day moving average. If either of those two criteria is true, the stock is in a downtrend. There is nothing more dangerous than a growth stock in a downtrend. A growth stock might go up 300% over three years, and then fall 80-95% once it enters a downtrend. This can happen even with major companies.

If a growth stock is trading above its 50-day moving average, and the 50-day moving average is trading above the 200-day moving average, I am happy to belong. If the stock is trading at new 52-week highs or all-time highs, that's even better. If a stock gaps up to new highs after a strong earnings report, that can be a great buy signal. Due to an anomaly called "Post-Earnings-Announcement Drift" (PEAD), a stock that has gapped up like this will tend to continue moving in the same direction for many days or even weeks. As a small investor, you can ride the wave, as larger institutional investors add to their positions over time, causing the stock to drift higher.

Understanding IPOs

IPO (Initial Public Offering) is viewed as a privately-owned business that has developed with a moderately modest number of investors, including early speculators like the originators, family, and companions alongside expert financial specialists, such as financial speculators or holy messenger speculators.

IPO furnishes the organization in collecting a great deal of cash and gives a more prominent capacity to develop and grow. The expanded straightforwardness and offer posting validity can likewise be a factor in helping it acquire better terms when looking for obtained assets.

The first sale of Bear parts of an association is esteemed through due underwriting steadiness. When an association opens to the world, the once-private offer ownership changes over to open ownership, and the present private financial specialists' offers become worth the open exchanging cost. Generally, the private to open advancement is a key time for private examiners to exchange out and win the benefits they were envisioning.

Private speculators may grasp their ideas in the open market or sell a piece or all of them for augmentations.

Meanwhile, the open market opens an enormous open entryway for some money-related authorities to buy shares in the association and contribute subsidizing to an association's financial specialists' worth. The open involves any individual or institutional monetary master who is enthusiastic about placing assets into the association.

As a rule, the number of offers the association sells and the expense for which offers sell are the making factors for the association's new financial specialists' worth. Financial specialists' worth is still controlled by examiners when it is both private and open. Anyway, with an IPO the speculators' worth augmentation will be on a very basic level with cash from the fundamental issuance.

Greatest IPOs

- Alibaba Group (BABA) in 2014 raising $25 billion
- American Insurance Group (AIG) in 2006 raising $20.5 billion

- VISA (V) in 2008 raising $19.7 billion
- General Motors (GM) in 2010 raising $18.15 billion
- Facebook (FB) in 2012 raising $16.01 billion

Lenders and the IPO Process

An IPO involves two areas. One, the pre-advancing time of the promotion. Two, the primary clearance of Bear itself. Exactly when an association is excited about an IPO, it will elevate to underwriters by mentioning private offers, or it can, in like manner, possess an open articulation to make interest.

The underwriters lead the IPO technique and are picked by the association. An association may pick one or a couple of agents to supervise different bits of the IPO technique agreeably. The lenders are related to each piece of the IPO due to constancy, document course of action, recording, publicizing, and issuance.

Steps to an IPO going with:

1. Underwriters present suggestions and valuations discussing their organizations, the best sort of

security to issue, offering esteem, the proportion of offers, and assessed time apportioning for the market promoting.

2. The association picks its underwriters and authoritatively agrees to ensure terms through an embracing understanding.

3. IPO gatherings are confined, including agents, legitimate counsels, guaranteed open clerks, and Securities and Trade Commission masters.

4. Information for the association is amassed for required IPO documentation. The S-1 Registration Statement is the basic IPO recording report. It has two areas: The arrangement and subtly held account information. The S-1 joins basic information about the ordinary date of the account. It will be adjusted as often as possible, all through the pre-IPO process. The included blueprint is in a similar manner refreshed interminably.

5. Marketing materials are made for pre-publicizing of the new Bear issuance.

Underwriters and authorities promote the offer issuance to measure solicitation and set up a last offering expense. Underwriters can revise their money-related examination all through the advancing technique. This can consolidate changing the IPO cost or issuance date as they see fit.

Associations figure out how to meet unequivocal open offers on essentials. Associations must hold quickly to both exchanges, posting essentials and SEC necessities for open associations.

A commonhold is a kind of money-related vehicle made up of a pool of funds assembled from various examiners to place assets into insurances, for instance, Bears, protections, cash market instruments, and multiple assets. Normal resources are worked by master money directors, who allocate the savings in favorable circumstances and attempt to convey capital increments or pay for the store's specialists. A typical store's portfolio is sorted out and kept up to match the endeavor targets communicated in its framework.

Regular backings give close to nothing, or individual specialist access to expertly supervised courses of action of esteems, bonds, and various securities. Each financial specialist, along these lines, takes an action, generally in the increments or hardships of the store. Normal resources put assets into many assurances, and execution is pursued as the modification in the outright market top of the save.

CHAPTER 5 ADVANCED ANALYSIS

After all the theories and information that you have been reading, market analysis is where your actual trading journey starts. The analysis is the process by which traders study the charts and use the knowledge in making decisions about their trades. We say that market analysis is not part of trading; it is the whole essence of trading.

This is another controversial context in the trading industry because traders never seem to agree on which, between the two major types of market analysis, is best. There are actually three types of market analyses. However, only two of them are popular since the third is usually a personal method. So, what are these types of chart analysis?

They are:

- Fundamental analysis
- Technical analysis

Let us look at what each one of them entails.

Fundamental Analysis

Fundamental analysis is a type of market analysis that tries to derive the underlying value of a financial instrument or asset by studying and assessing economic data. In this approach, the traders do not need to look at the charts to determine the future of the market. Rather, they seek all the relevant data about the instruments they are trading and then use the information to make their trades. Some of the economic data that traders look at closely include inflation, employment, GDP, exports, imports, interest rates, central banks' activities, and so on.

The objective of fundamentalists is to use economic reports as indicators to predict the overall conditions of the market. Out of this analysis, they hope to spot trading opportunities that promise high returns and minimum risk. In a nutshell, fundamentalist traders interpret present economic data and then use the information to decide whether an instrument is likely to gain or lose value in the future. For instance, they know that if a report comes out about Facebook launching a new product and the public being highly anticipative of it, the value of the Facebook share (stock) is likely to appreciate in the future. As such, they will buy stocks in anticipation of the growth in value.

Here are some of the economic data that fundamentalists focus on.

The Economy

The status of an economy directly affects the value of a country's currency, imports, exports, and other factors. If a country's economy is doing well, then its currency will grow stronger. Its exports will cost more, and the imports will be cheaper. For instance, when the price of oil increases, the value of all the currencies that produce and export the commodity will grow. Similarly, if the growth of an economy is reported to have dropped, the value of its currency and export commodities will decrease.

Political Stability

Political stability leads to increased confidence in the commodities or currencies of independent countries. On the other hand, political instability erodes investor confidence, leading to less investment and deterioration of economic performance. A good example was in 2018 when Facebook was entangled in the Cambridge Analytical scandal, where it was accused of interfering with the electoral process in Kenya, an East African country. On the first day of the report, Facebook shares lost close to $18 billion. By the time the scandal had stabilized, the company had lost over $134 billion. In this case, any trader that had sold the stock made a lot of money.

Government Policies

Government policies, such as interest rates, have significant effects on the general performance of currencies and commodities. When interest rates are increased, this curbs inflation and slows economic growth. Similarly, reducing interest rates stimulates economies by promoting investment. Other aspects, like fiscal policies, also affect the movement of the market. For example, high taxation slows economic performance and discourages business.

Observing Market Makers

There are traders who wait for the big players in the market to make their moves; then they will jump in and flow with the tide. They base their decisions on the assumption that since the big players have the ability to move the markets. If they can spot the big moves as they start, then they can reap big profits. Such traders will, therefore, place their focus on hedge funds, governments, central banks, and other huge financial institutions.

Reports and News Events

Do you remember 9/11? If so, then this point will be easy to understand. When the tragic news went live, the dollar plunged immediately. In about 5 days, the US economy had lost over $1.4 billion. In this case, anyone who had bought the EUR/USD would have made a lot of money. Similarly, any trader who had sold the USD/JPY would have made handsome profits as well.

Another event is when, in 2019, a Boeing 737 MAX crashed in Ethiopia a few months after a similar plane had crashed in Indonesia. Both flights killed all the passengers and crew.

Controversy emerged that the plane model was unsafe. In just a few days, the shares of Boeing sunk by 12%, which is close to $27 billion from the market. A trader who had analyzed this event and sold the Boeing stocks would have made a lot of money from the price decline.

Do you now understand how fundamental analysis works?

Advantages of Fundamental Analysis

- First, since fundamentalists seek to predict the movement of the markets before they happen, they can easily explain why a movement occurred. This fact alone is enough to increase one's predictive ability and profits.

- Second, studying economic data can help a trader to know the long-term position of price. In short, they can place trades and know where to anticipate the market to reach in the future. This improves their confidence when they have active trades.

- Third, due to the amount of data that is collected and analyzed, a trader gains a better understanding of the markets. As such, they can predict the markets more accurately and reduce guesswork.

- Disadvantages of Fundamental Analysis

- The biggest downside of fundamental analysis is that it lacks definite timing. A trader might know that the price of a stock will decline in the future, but they have no specific time when the fall will start. This is very risky when trading.

- Second, due to the lack of proper timing, this approach is not suitable for short-term trading, such as day trading or scalping. However, there are some types of fundamentals that can be used for day trading.

- The third disadvantage is that collecting too much economic data can lead to information overload. When this happens, the trader is unable to process the information. In the long run, they might make wrong decisions that can lead to losses.

- The final disadvantage is that interpreting economic information might vary. One trader might believe that a market will ascend while another interprets the same data in the opposite direction. A wrong interpretation can lead to inaccurate analysis and losses.

Technical Analysis

Technical analysis is the approach of analyzing the market using the movements of prices in the past. This approach is usually said to be more of an art than it is a science since it mostly uses observation, as opposed to complex formulas and derivations. This time, unlike in fundamental analysis, the trader relies on the charts found in the trading platforms to make their decisions. They do not need to try and interpret economic data but read what the charts are saying.

The most important tool in technical analysis is price data. Different timeframes will display different information, but, all the same, price data must be used to make the trading decisions. Technical analysis studies past and present action of price and helps the trader to predict the future behavior of the market. The behavior of price is studied using tools like the candlestick, lines, and bar charts that we saw earlier. This approach will work best where the instrument being traded, be it a stock, index, commodity, currency, futures, or option, has enough liquidity and is not susceptible to external influences.

Technical analysis is based on three major assumptions:

- First, that price behavior supersedes all other information, such as economic data. Technical traders firmly believe that the present behavior of price contains all the information about the market. Also, any new information is captured and shown immediately. Concisely, they do not believe so much in the fundamental approach.

- Second, that markets move in observable patterns. Technical traders assert that the market moves in patterns that can be observed and used to predict the future movement of prices. However, one has to be trained to observe the patterns when they form. The most-used observable pattern in trading is known as a 'trend.' A trend is a definite direction (up or down) that price seems to be following.

- Third, in the market, history will always be repeated. This assumption is closely related to the above point in that once a pattern has been observed, it can be expected to continue in a certain direction until the pattern has been completed. Repetition in price patterns can be seen in candlestick patterns, volume, chart formations, and momentum, to mention but a few.

Advantages of Technical Analysis

- By using charts, it is possible to choose any timeframe and focus on analyzing the market for a specific time. This is very important in day trading because we need timeframes that are less than one day to conduct our studies of price.

- Charts are visual tools; therefore, they enable us to see trends. Trends show the overall direction that the price is moving. In short, from a chart, we can see whether a market is bullish or bearish before deciding to buy or sell an instrument.

- The timing feature in the charts helps day traders to plan their working hours. They can decide when to work, when to break, or when to close their trades since they do not have to be carried over past midnight. In fundamental analysis, a trader's trading time is determined by external factors, such as the time when important data will be released.

- Technical analysis is preferred by many traders because it allows for the automation of concepts. Programmers can create automatic tools known as indicators and expert advisors (robots) to help with analyzing the market as well as entering or exiting trades.

- The other advantage of technical analysis is that it easily highlights important zones in the market. For example, you can tell where the market is likely to make a U-turn by looking at the charts. You will read more about this under Support and Resistance.

- Finally, compared to fundamental analysis, technical analysis is less consuming as the trader does not have to pursue different channels of information so they can make their trades. In the latter, we only need to look at the charts.

Disadvantages of Technical Analysis
- Charting is not as easy as it might sound. One reason is that different timeframes can give different signals. A 1-hour timeframe might predict a rising price,

while the 15-minute chart shows a falling price. Such occurrences can be confusing.

- There is another issue that is closely related to the above point, known as analysis paralysis. This is where a trader overanalyzes their charts until they get too confused to make a confident decision.

- Third, due to the presence of thousands of automated indicators and robots, different traders might interpret the market differently.

CHAPTER 6 MAKE MONEY WITH IPOS

Take Full Advantage of the Time

There are ways in which you can make money in the stock market even though you are there for the short-term, but the real benefit of the stock market is its compounding effect, and that can only happen in the long run. The money that is present in your account will grow as the value of the assets keeps increasing. This means that you are going to receive even more capital gains. So, with time, there is an exponential increase in the value of stocks.

But if you want this exponential factor to work in your favor, your investments in the stock market should start as early in your life as possible. So, the ideal way would be to start investing the moment you start earning, no matter how much it is.

An example should make it clearer to you as to what I am trying to explain. Let us say that you had put $1000 in your retirement account when you were of the age of 20. So, if you continue to work until the next 50 years, that is the age 70, and let us say that you did not put anything else into your retirement account. Even then, you will get something around $18,000 at the end of the term, assuming that there was a 6% rate of interest, which is quite moderate. But let us say that you made the initial deposit of $1000 60 years later, then you would be having only $800 in your account. So, you will be able to take full benefit of the power of compound interest only when you start your investment early.

Practice Investing Regularly

In the above paragraph, I already showed you how important time is when it comes to stock market investments, but time is not the only factor working here. If you decide not to save anything or anything reasonable, then even a decade couldn't turn your money into a handsome amount.

Let us say that instead of a one-time investment of $1000, you decide to contribute $1000 every year. And if you divide it, you will see that you have to save $20 each week to save $1000 in a year, and I think $20 is pretty easy to save. Now, let's assume that you start making the deposits when you are 20. Then, on your 70th birthday, you will be having $325,000 in your bank account. But instead of doing that, if you started saving from when you were 60 but invested $1000 every year, you'd have something around $15,000 in your account.

In fact, if you have a regular source of income, then you don't have to think about the payments—you can simply automate them, and they will be made on time. You can set a particular payment amount every week or every month.

Maintain a Portfolio That Is Diverse

Diversification is the key to making good profits in the market. There is a risk associated with every type of investment that you do. Sometimes, the companies that you are investing in now might be underperforming in the course of one year. But that is where diversification comes into play. If you don't invest all your money in one place, you will be safeguarding it against aspects that come out of the blue or are unplanned.

It is highly unlikely that when something happens, for example, a geopolitical event, all the stocks will be equally suffering. There will always be some stocks that are performing well while there will be others that are not performing that well. But if you have diversified your portfolio, then you will have better chances at hedging and mitigating the risk.

Take the Help of Some Professional

If you are a beginner, you should consider taking some professional help so that once you learn and you are in the trade, you can do everything by yourself. But before that, trading platforms can help you do all the research so that you are not wasting any of your time on that. It is true that your chances of loss cannot be mitigated even when you are using professional help, but when you have an expert working with you, you will automatically feel better and secure.

How to Succeed in the Stock Market?

If you want to be a successful investor, you have to understand that there is no shortcut to that—you simply have to give more effort. If you are someone who is following the feelings that your gut tells you that is not how you can be successful. In fact, that is how you are going to lose a lot of money. If you had guessed something and it turned out to be right, then you cannot call that a win. It was simply a coincidence. In order to succeed, you have to design full-proof strategies and also execute them in the right manner. Just like in a game of football, the team does not enter the field without a strategy; similarly, if you want to win in the stock market, don't set foot if you have not devised your strategy yet.

CHAPTER 7 EXCHANGE-TRADED FUNDS

Exchange-traded funds, or ETFs as they are often called, are a very exciting way to invest in the stock market. There are many advantages to an ETF as opposed to buying individual stocks. You can use exchange-traded funds to track major stock indexes, such as the Dow Jones Industrial Average, the S & P 500, small-cap stocks, midcap stocks, large-cap stocks, growth funds, value funds, real estate, gold, stocks in developing markets—you name it, it can be tracked with an ETF.

Essentially exchange-traded funds are like mutual funds, but they trade like stocks. So, you can just buy and sell shares the same way you'd buy and sell shares of Apple or Facebook. Unlike mutual funds, they are not actively managed by a financial guru so the fees are much lower. Also, while mutual funds only trade once a day, exchange-traded funds trade throughout the day like stocks because they are stocks.

ETFs Offer Automatic Diversity

When you invest in ETFs, you can choose between different indexes and sectors, among other things. So, you get automatic diversity because the fund is investing across a wide array of companies on your behalf. One of the most popular ETFs that are out there is SPY, which is a fund that has invested in the companies that make up the S & P 500. Imagine the difficulty you would have investing in all 500 companies, and then having to adjust the portfolio looking to weigh the fund to get more money invested into companies that performed better, and then taking companies in and out of your investments as the makeup of the S & P 500 changed. Of course, this would be a complete nightmare. So why not let someone else handle all of that for you? You can just invest in that fund and then let the market do the rest.

There are exchange-traded funds for many different sectors and investment goals. Finding the right ones for your situation will require a bit of research.

The Main Companies Offering ETFs

There are many investment firms that offer exchange-traded funds, but the main ones that you should spend your time looking at include:

- State Street SPDR
- Shares
- Vanguard.

While you are going to find that these companies offer funds that cover many of the same sectors and indexes of the markets, you are going to want to go head-to-head comparisons. Two funds that invest in the Dow Jones Industrial Average are not going to give you the same returns, for example. The reason is that while they are invested in the same companies, the weightings of the investments may be different. So, fund A may invest in companies 1, 2, 3, & 4 by putting 25% of the fund in each company, but fund B might put 30% in company 1, 40% in company 2, 15% in company 3, and 15% in company 4. Why would they do that? They might believe that companies 1 & 2 have much better growth potential.

So how are you going to find out which fund is better? By studying their past performance. Compare returns for different funds against each other and pick the one that you feel is best. Many times, the differences won't be stark. You will also want to have a look at fees associated with each fund, but for those coming from mutual funds you will be pleasantly surprised, the fees associated with exchange-traded funds are negligible.

Use Exchange-Traded Funds to Invest in... Everything

One of the things about exchange-traded funds is that you can put money into virtually anything. This makes them exciting and can offer an opportunity to build a real diversified portfolio but only by using stocks. For example, you can buy shares of VGIT, an exchange-traded fund offered by Vanguard. This fund invests in intermediate-term Treasuries—U.S. government-issued bonds. So rather than buying the bonds themselves, you can buy shares in this fund.

GLD is a fund offered by SPDR that invests in gold. So, you can invest in gold, but do it by owning shares of GLD, rather than going out and buying gold itself.

Let's take a look at funds that can help you build a diversified portfolio that suits your investment goals.

Remember—These Are Stocks

Although we are mentioning funds offered by different companies, you don't have to go to that company to invest. So, while you could open a Vanguard account, you don't have to. These funds all have stock tickers, you can just log into your brokerage account and simply buy shares in whatever fund you like.

A Look at Some Example Funds

For examples of large-cap funds, we'll have a look at offerings from Vanguard. Stock ticker VIG is a dividend appreciation fund. It tracks the "Dividend Achievers Select Index" on NASDAQ.

VUG, on the other hand, is a large-cap fund that tracks growth stocks. The ten largest holdings in this fund include Microsoft, Apple, Amazon, Alphabet (Google), Facebook, VISA, MasterCard, Home Depot, Boeing, and Comcast. Notice that by investing in this fund, you're automatically exposed to these ten companies while only having to make one investment.

When you look at each fund, you can also look at the weighting the fund has by sector. For example, this Vanguard fund has 34.9% invested in technology, 20% in consumer services, and 13.9% in industrials. Different funds that cover the same general goal will have different weightings by sector and different companies in their portfolios, although there may be a lot of overlap. These differences will impact the performance of each fund.

VTV is another large-cap offering by Vanguard. It is listed as a large-cap value fund. The holdings in this fund are quite different, reflecting the different goals of the fund. This time the top 10 holdings are: Berkshire Hathaway, JP Morgan Chase, Johnson & Johnson, Exxon Mobile,

Proctor & Gamble, Bank of America, Cisco Systems, Pfizer, and Intel.

VOT is a midcap growth fund managed by Vanguard. The holdings on this fund include Roper Technologies, Red Hat, and Twitter, among others. Vanguard considers it to be in their highest risk category, but if you are looking to add more aggressive growth to your portfolio, it's an option to consider as opposed to making the investments yourself. Vanguard also has a few small-cap funds. You can also invest in microcap ETFs, IWC is a microcap fund offered by shares.

Tracking index funds is one of the best ways to use ETFs. We've already mentioned SPY, but there are many other stock indexes that you can track to invest in different areas. Some of the other index funds and sectors you can track with ETFs are:

- NASDAQ Composite Index: Mostly technology stocks traded on NASDAQ.
- Wilshire 5000: Designed to track the entire stock market. Not as popular as SPY.

- S & P Midcap 400, Russell MidCap, Wilshire US Midcap: Track midcap companies.

- Russell 2000: Tracks small-cap companies.

- Sector funds: Track energy, healthcare, finance, utilities, etc.

- Emerging markets.

- Real estate.

- Corporate bonds, including junk bonds.

- Precious metals, including gold and silver.

ETFs and Dividends

One question many people have does ETFs pay dividends. The answer is yes, they do. So, if you are looking for a way to build an income investment portfolio based on dividends, exchange-traded funds can be part of that process. Dividends are paid out quarterly. The proportion of dividends you receive will depend on what percentage of the fund you own. So, if you own 0.1% of the fund, you will receive 0.1% of the dividends.

ETFs Make It Easy

One of the nice things about using ETFs to build a diversified portfolio hitting different market capitalizations, sectors, and so forth, is that you can diversify your portfolio without having to study the details on dozens of stocks and companies. Of course, different things appeal to different people; some people want to put the time into studying companies and their performance, while others will prefer the hands-off nature of ETFs.

What I like to do is mix it up, so I will invest 50% in individual stocks, and the other 50% of my stock market investing goes to ETFs. There is no reason to be exclusive one way or another unless you really want to.

CHAPTER 8 FUTURES

In futures trading, the buyer required buying, or the seller needed to sell the underlying securities at the price that has set, no matter the current price in the market is or what the expiry date is. The underlying assets comprise physical commodities and other instruments of financing. They are standardized as well for facilitating trading on a futures exchange. You can use futures for speculation of trade or hedging.

Futures, also known as futures contracts, permit the traders to set the price of the underlying security or asset. All such agreements come along with dates of expiry and set prices that are determined upfront. Futures generally identify using the month of expiry. For instance, a gold futures contract from December will expire in December. While trading futures, there are various types of contracts that you are most likely to come across.

- Stock futures, for example, the S&P Index

- Commodity futures, for example, natural gas, crude oil, wheat, and corn
- U.S. Treasury futures related to bonds and various other products
- Precious metal futures for silver and gold
- Currency futures including pound and euro.

It is essential to identify the differences between futures and options. Contracts of options provide the holder with an overall right for selling or buying the underlying security at the date of expiration. The holder of futures contracts is obliged to fulfill all the contract terms.

Pros of Futures Trading

- The investors can use up contracts of futures for speculating right on the direction in the set price of the underlying assets.

- Companies have the chance of hedging the raw material price or the products sold by them for protecting themselves from adverse movements of the cost.

- The contracts of futures need a deposit of only a portion of the amount of the contract with the broker.

Cons of Futures Trading

- Investors have the risk of losing more than the starting margin amount as futures use up leverage.

- Investing in contracts of futures might lead a company that hedged to miss the favorable movements of the price.

- The related margins might act as a double-edged sword. The gains will amplify, and so will be the losses.

The market of futures uses high leverage. Leverage means that a trader of futures is not required to give in 100% amount of the contract value at the time of entering any trade. Instead, the broker will need an initial amount of margin, which includes a part of the total cost of the contract. The amount that will be held by a broker can differ relying on the contract size, the terms and conditions of the broker, and the investor's creditworthiness.

The exchange where the trading of futures takes place will determine whether the contract can be cash-settled or meant for physical delivery. Any corporation can enter into a contract of physical delivery for locking in the commodity price that they need for production. But, most trades of futures are from all those traders who speculate on the trades. Contracts are either netted or closed out. The difference between the closing price of the trade and the cost of the original trade is settled by cash.

Speculation of Futures

A contract of futures permits a trader to speculate on the movement direction of the price of a commodity. If a trader purchases a contract of futures and the commodity price rises and starts trading much above the actual cost of the contract at the date of expiry, the trader will be making a profit. Before the expiry date, the long position would be unwound with a selling trade for a similar amount at the present price, effectively closing the extended position. The difference between the contract prices will be cash-settled in the brokerage account of the investor. No form of physical products will be changing hands. But the trader might also incur a loss if the price commodity turns out to be lower than the cost of purchase that has specified in the contract of futures.

The speculators will also be able to take a sell speculative or short position if they think that the price of the underlying security will be falling. If the asset price declines, the trader will be taking an offset place for closing the futures contract. Once again, the difference will get settled at the expiry date of the futures contract. An investor can make a profit when the price of the underlying asset is below the cost of the contract and will incur a loss if the present rate is more than the price of the contract.

It is essential to note that margin trading will permit a more significant position than the actual amount held by the account of the brokerage. As a result, investing in margin can improve the percentage of profits but can also maximize the losses. For example, when a trader has a brokerage account balance of $5,000, and he is in a trade for a position of $50,000 in crude oil. If the oil price moves in the opposite direction of the trade, the trader will incur a loss that can even exceed the $5,000 margin amount of the account. In such a case, the broker will be making a margin call for additional funds that need to deposit for covering the losses of the market.

Futures Hedging

Futures can use up for hedging the movement of the price of the underlying security. The primary goal here is to prevent losses from the inherent nature of unfavorable changes in price rather than speculating. Most of the companies that opt for hedges are producing or using the underlying security. For instance, a farmer of corn can start using futures to lock in a selling price for their crop. By doing this, he can potentially cut down the risk and guarantee that he can receive a fixed amount of pay. If by chance, the corn price falls, the company will be gaining on the hedges for offsetting the losses from selling the crop in the market. With such a form of loss and gain offsetting one another, hedging can effectively lock in a high price in the market.

Futures Regulation

The markets of futures regulate by the CFTC or Commodity Futures Trading Commission. CFTC is a form of a federal agency that was set up by Congress in the year 1974 to ensure integrity in the market price of futures. It also included the prevention of abusive practices related to trading, regulation of the brokerage firms that are related to futures trading, and prevention of fraud.

Example of Futures Trading

Suppose a trader is willing to speculate on the crude oil price by entering a position in the contract of futures in May. He enters the position with the expectation that the crude oil price will go up by the end of the year. The crude oil futures of December traded at $50, and the trader fixes in the contract at that price. As crude oil is traded in the increment of 1,000 barrels, the trader is now holding a position that is worth $50,000 in crude oil ($50 x 1,000 = $50,000). But the trader is only required to pay out a part of the total amount upfront, the initial amount margin that is needed to deposit with the related broker.

In the period between May to December, the crude oil price will fluctuate exactly as the futures contract price. In case the price of crude oil turns out to be too volatile, the broker might ask out for extra funds that need to deposit into the account of margin. In December, the expiry date of the futures contract is approaching, which is the third Friday of that month. The overall price of crude oil rose to $65. Now, the trader sells out the original futures contracts for exiting his position. The total difference will be cash-settled. They will earn a total of $15,000, excluding the commissions and fees of the broker ($65 - $50 =$15, $15 x 1,000 = $15,000).

But, if the price of crude oil came down to $40 in place of rising to $65, the trader will be losing $10,000 ($50 - $40 =$10, $10 x 1,000 = $10,000).

Futures are an excellent form of investment when appropriately used. It would help if you determined the market conditions accurately for gaining profits.

CHAPTER 9   MUTUAL FUNDS

I have to admit that I invested in mutual funds late in the game even though it is an investment opportunity that works very well for beginner investors. Many people believe that there is an ideal age for investing and if you have missed that gate then all is lost. That is not true. I know of investors who started their careers in their 40s and still went on to achieve their financial goals even though the window for doing so had shrunk. The key is to get a grip on your finances and take a good, hard look at your current portfolio to find the ways it needs improving.

That was why I considered mutual funds. There were holes in my financial portfolio that needed filling and mutual funds fit my needs, something I realized after I did some investigating. However late I was, I am so glad that I turned to mutual fund investing because any investor who would like a balanced portfolio understands that investing in mutual funds is a great way of spreading risk while still earning the wealth status desired. Still, mutual funds can seem complicated to understand right out of the gate. I too scratched my head when I contemplated investing in them at first and that may have been why I waited so long to invest in them. Today, I understand that the fear was unfounded and mutual funds are simple to understand once you look a little bit deeper. The entire idea of mutual funds centers on investing money with other people toward a common goal.

The formal definition of a mutual fund states that it is a pool of money collected from individual investors, companies, and other entities as a way to invest in the market and spread risk so that it does not fall on the individual investors, company, or other entity.

To facilitate this collective investment, a fund manager is hired to invest the funds collected from the investors, companies, or other entities. The fund manager invests this money based on the type of mutual fund specified by the group to meet their goals. The intervention of a fund manager allows the fund to be professionally managed.

As an investor in this sort of transaction, this person gets a stake of ownership in the fund and whatever profit that it makes.

Types of Mutual Funds

There are two basic types of mutual funds and they are called closed-ended funds and open-ended funds. Below, we will discuss the characteristics of both types of mutual funds and the subcategories that fall within them.

Closed-Ended Funds

Closed-ended mutual funds have a fixed maturity date and allow investments only in the initial stages of developing the fund. Due to the introduction of a fixed maturity date, investors cannot withdraw from the fund until that time arrives.

There are two types of closed-ended mutual funds and they are called capital protection funds and fixed maturity plans. Capital protection funds consist of getting income from a balanced exposure to both equity and debt. This mutual fund type is largely towards debt securities and as such, investments are made heavily in bonds, certificates of deposits, and T-bills to name a few. Investing in a capital protection fund offers a great amount of risk protection compared to other types of mutual funds. They are also beginner-friendly and offer a great way to gain experience in equity investing. The negative part of capital protection funds is that returns on this type of mutual fund are limited and investors are not allowed to exit the fund before the maturity date arrives.

Just like with capital protection funds, investing in fixed maturity plans mainly uses instruments such as bonds and certificates of deposits. This is done in an effort to eliminate interest rate fluctuations that can be experienced in debt markets. The locked-in maturity dates of such mutual funds are typically varied between 30 days and 5 years.

Due to the nature of fixed maturity plans, they are often confused with fixed deposits but they differ from bank fixed deposits in that they do not carry components of equity borrowing. An investor may be interested in a fixed maturity plan if he or she wishes to generate steady returns over the fixed period specified while enjoying the protection against market price fluctuations.

Open-Ended Funds

Unlike closed-ended mutual funds, open-ended mutual funds allow investors to buy and sell at any time. There is no fixed maturity date or investment period attached to such mutual funds. Open-ended mutual funds are placed into four categories. These four categories are:

- Debt or income mutual funds. These are low-risk and low-return mutual fund types that allow investments in treasury bills and bonds. They are a good option for investors looking for a low-risk option.

- Equity or growth mutual funds. These types of mutual funds are with the intention of generating substantial income, retaining capital gains, and investment in equity stocks.

- Liquid or money market mutual funds. These have a short maturity date of only about 90 days and investments are made in fixed income securities like short-term bank certificates of deposit and treasury bills. These are highly liquid securities.

- Balanced mutual funds. These mutual funds allow an aggressive investment that is curtailed by caution as it allows a balance between investment in fixed income securities and equity funds.

How to Invest in Mutual Funds

Before you wade into the pool of mutual funds, you need to determine what you would like to achieve out of using that investment tool. Common goals include running a stable income during retirement allowing assets to grow in value in the process known as capital appreciation. Your goals allow you to draw a map that allows you to get to where you want to be. Having these financial goals will allow you to know what type of mutual fund would work best with the direction that you are going and how much money you would like to start with. The wonderful thing about mutual funds is that the investment amount is relatively low in comparison to many other investment strategies. Mutual fund investing also allows for the investment in a vast and diverse range of underlying securities that can easily be converted into cash.

Another important consideration that must be determined when investing in mutual funds is the timeline with which you would like to work. That again ties in with your goals so that you know in how many months or years you would like your investment to achieve its financial objective.

The amount of risk that you would like to take on is also a consideration when it comes to choosing the right mutual fund for you. As with anything else in the financial world, the mutual funds with the greatest potential for returns are also the ones that are riskiest to invest in. One of the riskier types of mutual funds to invest in is stock funds while mutual funds that generate lower returns like money market funds carry less risk.

The types of mutual funds that you can invest in are wide and varied and this list includes the three basic types that most investors start with. These three are called stock funds, bond funds, and money market funds. All three of these are categorized as open-ended mutual funds.

Stock funds allow the investment in stocks as the name suggests. As mentioned earlier, stock funds generally have a higher level of risk associated with them because the potential for returns is also typically higher than with most other types of mutual funds. This higher potential for returns and the associated risk are the result of the volatility of stock prices on the market. Therefore, this type of mutual fund is typically sought by investors willing to accept a higher level of risk as they seek aggressive capital appreciation. These types of investors are also typically willing to see the return on their investment over a longer timeline.

Bonds are a debt instrument and as such, bond funds allow investors to leverage their money into a pool to become a lender to a separate entity, which will have responsibility for paying the monies lent back into the fund with periodic interest applied. The risks associated with bond funds are generally lower than stock funds but this risk varies depending on the type of bond invested in. For example, investing in companies with low credit ratings or investing in long-term bonds are riskier compared to investing in short-term bonds or bonds associated with more stable entities such as the government.

Money market funds are lower-risk mutual fund investments suitable for the short-term such as if the investor is expecting a yield in 3 years or less. Money market funds typically offer lower rates compared to stock funds or bond funds but traditionally, they offer a steady income. The instruments that are typically invested in with a mutual fund of this type are highly liquid instruments such as cash equivalent securities and cash. Instruments that are highly liquid have very low risk attached to them and therefore, the potential for high yield is lowered in reflection.

Mutual fund purchases can be done directly through a mutual fund company or a bank. Buying mutual funds is facilitated through a brokerage firm as well but unlike stocks, which are purchased in shares, mutual funds are purchased in dollar amounts. In order to purchase mutual funds needs to be facilitated by opening an account with any of the institutions that you choose to purchase the mutual fund through. In this day and age, purchasing mutual funds is not a tedious process and can be done online or over the phone if you do not feel like dealing with an in-person transaction. Purchasing the mutual fund is done by indicating the amount that you would like to spend and what mutual fund you would like to purchase. It is as easy as that and I still mentally kick myself for not investing in mutual funds sooner.

There is a feature offered by some brokerage firms that is called an automatic investment plan that allows an investor to periodically invest a certain amount on autopilot. This can be a consideration if you want to take some of the headwork out of your mutual fund investment strategy.

The Benefits of Investing in Mutual Funds

One of the biggest advantages of investing in mutual funds is that the investment is handled by the expert fund manager who has an understanding of how the market works and who knows the best techniques that will allow for maximum gain of the collective investment.

Other benefits include:

- Investment in mutual funds can be done in installments or in lump sums.
- Investing in mutual funds does not require large sums of money for investing.
- Risk is spread by being divided among the many participants.
- Risk is minimized by funds being invested in different securities such as stocks and bonds.
- Investors are allowed to choose between low, medium, and high-risk mutual funds to adhere to their comfort levels when it comes to risk management.
- Open-ended mutual funds are typically highly liquid.

CHAPTER 10 HOW TO MINIMIZE LOSSES AND MAXIMIZE GAINS WITH STOCKS?

When it comes to money, what matters most is not how much you earn, but how well you handle what you have. Being able to enhance the cash you have considered is the hallmark of real money management, and also one of the most efficient ways to accomplish this is to invest in stocks. Market researchers assert that for five years, buying stocks can produce, at a minimum, a 20% return.

To earn money by investing in stocks, an individual should first know the rules of trading. These rules are mandatory and are regulated to secure both financiers and the trading industry itself. Considering that somebody can face prosecution for bending or damaging these policies, investors might find it helpful to find out more about the regulations on the specified website to have more understanding.

There are two primary means you can buy stocks.

The first is investing, which is where a specific search for long-term gains in the stocks market, and purchases companies that offer potentially higher growth. This strategy calls for in-depth research of firms to determine the best ones to invest in, yet brings relatively little risk. The downside is that not everybody has the time or the ability to recognize all the financial details of a company.

Another style is called trading, which is where the investor tries to benefit from the ups and downs of the stock market. The success of this approach will depend partly on the personality of the investor, as the short-term volatility of the stock market can be stressful. While this design of trading can stock considerable returns in a short space of time, it's not for the fainthearted.

Before investing, think of a strategy that includes plainly defined objectives, creates a personal risk profile and establishes a long-time for investing. Knowing when to sell is as vital as understanding when to buy. Don't time the market, but enter it in stages, benefiting from the market volatility.

Stock market investment has some kind of fundamental threats in it; this kind of investment is one of how you can make some money. You might start to spend in stocks when you are young to be safe from risks entailed in the stock market.

Securities Market Manipulation—How to Protect Yourself

Stock exchange control is among the most significant problem in today's financial world. Despite having Obama's determined relocate to stop such acts, we need to deal with the truth. No matter how risk-free and safe we think the market is, there are always those higher up that will abuse their power and use it to their benefit.

For amateur traders, this is somewhat frustrating. Once it starts looking stronger, hands begin reeling costs in, and by the end of the day's close, the market back to where it began.

These include:

1. Spend a week examining price patterns and see when bigger great deals of volume have been available during the day. These are probably the more significant players attempting their hand to trick you.

2. During the day, be careful of Amateur hr. This is the first hr of the day when the brand-new novice

investors come in and coldly start buying every little thing.

3. Always scale into settings and out of positions. These will reduce loss and optimize your gains.

4. Avoid chop time. This is a quiet time in the market do not trade it. Cut time got its name in the old days by amateur investors that got their accounts cut to items when they tried to buy during lunchtime in the market.

5. Always set your stop losses in the market in case something goes wrong. Take it on the chin, get up, and you will live to fight one more day.

6. Make sure you never trade alone. Always work with investors that are better than you. This will help you become much better. With the control that takes place, you will need all eyes on you.

7. Get a mentor. Get somebody who knows the ropes to educate you about how the manipulators work their magic during the day on the stock exchange. This can save you a lot of distress, but most notably, it can conserve you from losing your account.

Leave Strategies That Lock in Profits and/or Minimize Losses

When developing a departure technique, there are three things that we should take into consideration.

1. How long are we intending on being in this trade?
2. How much risk are we willing to take?
3. At what cost point do we want to exit?

The answers are:

Set revenue targets to be hit in some months, which will certainly lessen the number of trades you make.

Develop tracking stop-loss factors that enable earnings to be secured periodically to limit the disadvantage capacity. Bear in mind, the primary objective of any type of trade should be to protect resources.

Take revenues in increments over time to minimize volatility while liquidating.

Allow for volatility to make sure that you maintain your trades to a minimum.

Create leave approaches based on essential aspects geared in the direction of the longer term. Let's claim you love the company model of ISRG, and you think the company's growth possibility to be enormous. In this situation, you may wish to hold the stock long-term and create a price target based on future income development. Nevertheless, if you are in a trade temporarily, you should not bother yourself with these things because they do not matter on a short-term basis. Too many short-term investors try to trade on fundamentals, and it does not make good sense to do that. Fundamentals only work in the event you wish to invest in a company as opposed to trading their stock.

Set near-term revenue targets that perform at favorable times to make the best use of earnings. Right here are some common implementation points:

- Pivot Points (A technical sign acquired by determining the numerical average of specific stocks high, low, and closing rates)
- Fibonacci/Gann degrees
- Trend line breaks.

The secret is to learn a system that helps you and one that creates solid stop-loss points that get rid of stocks that do not work in the right manner.

How Much Threat Are We Willing to Take?

This will certainly establish the size of our trade and the type of stop-loss we need to use. Those who desire less risk tend to develop tighter stops, and those who presume more risk offer the position more area to maneuver or work as they state.

It is also essential to set your stop-loss points so that they are protected from being set off by average market volatility. This can be done in several ways.

The beta indication can give you an excellent concept of how volatile the stock is relative to the market in general, but these are great for longer-term traders that can endure 10% losses. An example would certainly be if the beta is within 0 and 2; after that, you will be risk-free with a stop-loss point at 10-20% lower than where you got the stock.

Where Do We Desire to Obtain Out?

You may ask, why would you want to establish a take-profit factor or limitation order where we sell when our stock is doing well? The answer is. Ideally, we do not intend to do something like this, but there are times when it for your benefit. Lots of people are crazily connected to their placements and hold the stocks when the underlying basics or technical of the profession have changed. The only thing excellent about a limit sell order is the reality that it takes the feeling out of the trade. It either strikes your sell restriction order, or it hits your stop-loss point, and you can deal with your service after you enter your decrees and not have to stress over how your position is doing while you are away. If you are to sell this way, your exit point must be evaluated at a critical price level such as rate resistance, trend line resistance, or other technological aspects on the chart such as particular Fibonacci levels.

Leave strategies and various other money monitoring techniques can significantly improve your trading by getting rid of emotion and reducing risk. Before you enter a trade, take into consideration the inquiries noted above.

CHAPTER 11 FACTORS AFFECTING THE STOCK MARKET

The stock market can be described by one special element; it is called change. It continues to change due to so many forces and influences. The volatility can be brought about by a number of issues. Take note that the following factors are not exhaustive. They are not the only factors that can affect the movement of stocks in the market but have a role in the performance of stocks.

Economy

The economy is very much connected with the stock market. In fact, you can tell if the economy is doing well by looking at the stock market. States that have a good economy tend to also have a stable stock market.

Political Events

As can be expected, the stock market cannot escape the influence of politics. For example, when JFK was assassinated, the U.S. stock market sank since investors were hesitant to place any investment. And, since stocks and bonds operate within a legal framework, the state's power to enact laws can also affect the stock market. After all, laws can directly affect many businesses.

Media

The media greatly affects the stock market. Due to the attention that the media can bring, it can either make or break companies, as well as their stocks. Media announcements can also cause lots of reactions, which can significantly affect the volatility of certain stocks.

Supply and Demand

As can be expected in any business, supply and demand

affect the stock market. When the prices are low (high supply), then many investors make a buy-in order, thereby creating demand. Then, the price will rise, and supply decreases. However, once the price gets too high, the demand drops, and the investors wait and look for other opportunities. Demand and supply will always fluctuate. Once in a while, they may appear balanced. Part of their nature is a continuous fluctuation, which also affects the stock market.

Natural Disasters

As ironic as this may be, natural disasters tend to be beneficial to the stock market. This is because right after a natural disaster, people tend to spend lots of money on their rebuilding efforts and projects. Also, while natural disasters may damage the market for some time, they mostly initiate growth.

Investors Themselves

Each moment an investor purchases stock or makes a sell, it affects the stock market. Now, just imagine how many investors engage in the same activity. For example, when certain investors have confidence in a particular stock, they purchase the said stock, and its price naturally increases. Say, due to the increased value, it manages to draw attention and other people also start buying the same stocks. Now, when it has reached its peak and the confidence in the stock begins to wane, the market simply collapses and fails.

Marketing Hype

It is so easy to promote something these days. You can easily share something with the world with just a few clicks of a mouse. Hence, many people have taken advantage of this by marketing some stocks in order to raise their value. In the stock market, the more attention the stocks draw, the higher their prices tend to increase. These days, there are people who promote themselves as "experts."

World Events

World events, regardless of whether good or bad, affect the stock market. They simply draw so much attention, and issues like having a change of leadership, international relations, and others, can either cause a boost in the market or cause it to panic.

News

News especially that relating to businesses and the economy, can dramatically affect the stock market. Depending on the news, it can cause the value of stocks to rise or fall. Company news and announcements can also affect how investors analyze the market. If there is a likelihood of a company being successful, there will be an improvement in the performance of its stock and thus experiences growth.

Deflation

When prices decrease, then companies also experience lower profits, which also tend to create less economic activity. The prices of stocks may then drop, which will compel investors to share their shares and simply move to a more secure investment like bonds.

These are some factors influencing a stock's volatility. It is suggested that you learn to understand just how these forces influence the performance of certain stocks, as well as market behavior.

When Should You Sell Your Stocks?

An important element in making money with stocks is to know when to sell them. Many investors lose their money not only because of choosing the wrong stocks to invest in. Sometimes, they lose their money by holding on for so long to what once was a good stock.

When the Company Shows Signs of Weakening

When a company experiences changes that are likely to weaken its performance, it is the right moment to sell the shares before it is too late. For example, when the sales of a company which have shown good performance through the years suddenly face a significant decline, then it is time for you to reconsider whether or not it is still a good investment to keep your stocks in that company.

When The Company Removes Dividends

If there no dividends at all or show signs of instability, it may act as an indication that the company is headed to no good. This is a serious red signal. When the situation occurs, you are advised to sell your stocks immediately.

When You Attain Your Objective

Many times, you can avoid losing your money by not being greedy. Some investors decide to sell their stocks once they are already satisfied with their profit. For example, say you buy certain stocks at $10 per share, and your aim is to get a

50% profit. If the value of those stocks increases and reaches $15 (50% increase), then you sell the stocks right away. Avoid greediness and hope for it to reach $20 or even $16. By doing so, you get to minimize your risks, which also minimizes your losses.

Factors to Consider While Choosing Stocks

You have to take time to perform an analysis to select the right stocks to invest in. A wrong choice of stock can make you lose a lot of money and be a wastage of your precious time. Get more information about a given company you have an interest in and scrutinize their financial reports to know if you can invest with them. It is best to understand all the financial information you get about a company before you make the final investment decision.

It is important to choose to invest in a business that is doing well. You will be in a position to enjoy the peace of mind that your investment will not go to waste and that you will enjoy the gains. To know if a company is performing well, be keen with a number of clues that include:

- The company's profit margin

- A company's return on equity

- Past performance and expected growth

- Its historic rate of earnings growth compared to its peers

- The debts that the company has

The debt-to-equity ratio means taking the company's debt and dividing it by shareholder equity. The lower the percentage is, the better and safer your investment will be.

Here are some factors that will help you make the right choice of stock to invest in:

- Effective management of the business—It is a pertinent issue to study. However, not many investors are able to access how effective business management is, therefore they do not consider this. Return on equity and the income shareholders earn per their investments is a great indication of how the business management uses the money investors have invested in the business. A business with a return on equity of 5% or more is a good one to consider investing in.

- Stocks from a suitable business sector—It is important to choose the industry sectors where you want to invest wisely. Some sectors do better than others, which is why this is important. Do not concentrate on one sector of the economy; this can, in fact, be risky for your investment. When you are diversifying, only go for stocks in the leading industry sectors to ensure that at least all your stocks will be performing well. If, after some time, you will want to invest more money, you will invest in the sector that is doing better than the others. If there is a sector that is not doing well and you have already invested in it, you can always withdraw your investment as soon as possible, then reinvest the money in a better-performing sector.

- The growing profits—Consider investing with a firm showing the potential for profits. Go for a company whose earnings per share growth is steady and at least 5% or more. This is what will assure you that you will be getting some money at the end of every year for as long as you will be investing in that company.

- The size of the company—It is riskier to invest in small companies than in large ones. The big companies that have already established themselves already know how to survive in the market, therefore, it is hard for such companies to go down. That is why they are the best to invest in. If possible, avoid penny stocks unless if you are willing to deal with all the risks involved. To be guaranteed regular returns, buy stocks of big businesses.

- Manageable debt—A business can borrow money in order to build itself but too much debt is not good for the business. Ensure you have information on this before investing your money so that you will know if the debt per capita ratio is healthy or not. A rate of 0.5 or less is a good one but if it is more then there will be a problem thereafter. A business that is in debt will not be able to compensate its investors and you might end up losing all your investment in the repayment of those debts.

- Dividend payments—Companies that return part of their profits to the investors in terms of dividends are good companies to invest in. A dividend payment of 2% or more is a good one to consider, therefore, this is an important factor too. Dividends are important to investors. This is where the return on your investment on an annual basis comes in.

- Stocks with sufficient liquidity—These are stocks that can easily be sold out if you no longer want to continue owning them. Some stocks are hard to sell, and these will give you a lot of problems when you finally want to sell them off. It is good to consider investing in stocks that will allow you to sell your position as fast as you want when the need arises.

CHAPTER 12 MAJOR STOCK EXCHANGES

The stock market has a few major stock exchanges that are worth talking about in more detail. These markets are where most of the volume and liquidity (money) will be, thus the markets that have the most movement and profit to offer.

The Four Major Exchanges

NYSE

The New York Stock Exchange sees about $13.4 trillion in movement a day. The NYSE is the largest stock exchange in the world in terms of trade volume. It is also located in a physical location like all stock exchanges. The NYSE regulates stocks, commodities, and other product exchanges. Companies from around the world list their IPOs on the NYSE to gain the attention of investors. Companies can be locally listed on their country's exchange and then launch on the NYSE when they become large enough to sustain the interest in their shares. Companies can only be listed on one exchange at a time to avoid regulatory issues, and some countries do not allow their companies to list on the NYSE. Any stock listed on the NYSE can be purchased by traders to make a profit and earn dividends.

In North America, there is more than one exchange, like the Philadelphia exchange and Toronto. However, it is the NYSE, Dow index, and NASDAQ that get the most media.

Tokyo Stock Exchange

Japan's stock exchange is the TSE, and it sees $3.8 trillion in movement per day, although in 2014, it was listed as $4 trillion. The Tosho (TSE) is considered the third-largest in terms of market cap, but the number of companies listed is only 2,292 making it the fourth largest for the number of companies listed on the exchange. In 2012, the TSE merged with Osaka Securities Exchange to become the JPX or Japan Exchange Group. The exchange runs from 9 am to

11:30 am and from 12:30 to 3 pm during the weekdays. These are hours based on the Asian time zone.

LSE

The London Stock Exchange dealt with approximately $3.6 trillion market movement for the day before 2014. The LSE was formed in 1801 and, as of 2014, had $6.06 trillion as a market cap. The London Stock Exchange is considered the second-largest by market cap data; however, it is behind the NASDAQ in terms of overall size. The LSE has merged with certain exchanges like Borsa Italiana, MTS, Turquoise, NASDAQ Bids, and there is a proposed merger with TMX Group. The LSE has primary markets with premium listed main market companies, which are the biggest UK markets. There is the Alternative Investment Market for smaller companies, a professional securities market, and a specialist fund market. The LSE is open daily, on weekdays from 8 am to 4:30 pm, GMT.

Euronext

This is the European Stock Exchange. It was smaller, dealing with only $2.9 trillion in market movement per day before the split with the NYSE. In 2015, the exchange started seeing closer to $3.7 trillion as a market cap. This was after Euronext made a public offering to become a separate entity. The market offers equities, exchange-traded funds, bonds, derivatives, commodities, warrants and certificates, and indices. It was established as an exchange in Amsterdam, London, Brussels, Paris, and Lisbon, as well as part of the Intercontinental Exchange.

Other Popular and Major Exchanges

In this list, you will see three other major exchanges, which are popular in certain markets like Asian stock investments. They are listed because they have a higher market cap in comparison to other exchanges that exist around the world.

Shanghai Stock Exchange

Shanghai is another Asian market that sees a high volume of $2.7 trillion.

Hong Kong Stock Exchange

Hong Kong has the same amount of traffic as the Shanghai Market.

Toronto Stock Exchange

Toronto is home to Canada's stock exchange. The market cap for this exchange is $2.2 trillion.

Stock Market Performance and Indexes

The NASDAQ and Dow Jones are two important indexes to discuss and determine market performance. Each needs to be explained to help you understand how the stock market works.

NASDAQ

The NASDAQ is a stock exchange that also offers options trading. It is an exchange that was the first electronic stock market, which lowered the spread charged to investors. The spread is the difference between the buy and sell price and is where most brokerage firms make their money. The NASDAQ offers a premarket period to fit into the London Stock Exchange part of the trading system. These hours are 4 am to 9:30 am EST and then from 9:30 am to 4 pm for the normal trading session. There is a post-market session that fits in the Asian time zone trading period, and those hours are 4 pm to 8 pm.

The NASDAQ has market tiers: small, mid, and large-cap. They are referred to as the capital, global, and global select market, respectively.

The stock exchange sees $9.6 trillion in daily movement. Approximately 3,600 companies are listed on the exchange. Investors can do more on the NASDAQ with options trading than on other exchanges. Options are a complicated process that you will want advanced stock market investing information to understand. You need to know it is an exchange with a different list of companies than the NYSE that may offer you room to grow into options trading.

The Dow Jones

It is a stock market index that measures the price of a specific unit of the stock market. It is computed based on selected stocks based on an average of the price of these shares. Investors use it to figure out the market movement and market health based on the average prices of top companies. Mutual funds and exchange-traded funds tend to use this type of index to track what the funds will do or have done in reacting to news and economic data. The Dow Jones was the first stock market index to be started. It was devised by Charles Dow in 1896. Edward Jones was his partner and a statistician. They weigh 30 components that have to do with traditional industries.

Stock market investors will use the Dow Jones to determine the performance of a specific industry sector for American companies and the overall weighting of the USA's economic stability. The Dow Jones is not meant to be influenced by economic reports or corporate reports, but by price movement alone.

You can use the Dow Jones for ETF, leverage, short funds, futures contracts, and options contracts.

When you hear media experts talking about the market going up or down by a certain number of "points," they are usually talking about the Dow Jones index computation.

CONCLUSION

Thank you for making it to the end. Remember that risk management is paramount. Always stick to your per-trade risk figures and do not deviate from this no matter how attractive the setup might seem. Remember, the odds of success of a slam dunk-looking setup and one that looks like a dog's dinner are the same. The market does not care about how pretty your setup is, so you shouldn't either. If the underlying conditions are fulfilled, you should execute your setup in the correct manner.

Your analysis should always begin with the technical market situation which is the order flow distribution and the trend or range situation. Often you will deal with trends with close to equal participation from both sides of the market. This should tell you that a reversal is probably imminent, and you should adjust accordingly.

Support and resistance will play an important role in determining where you ought to place your strike prices. Remember to evaluate support and resistance levels from an order flow perspective, instead of looking at every single available level on the chart. Look at the order flow characteristics the preceding time price made it there and compare it to the current order flow to get a feel for whether the level will hold or not.

Screening stocks is a straightforward matter if you follow the process outlined here. Compare the sector performance to the overall market performance to narrow down which sectors you ought to focus on. Once this is done, repeat the same process with individual stocks to select the best to speculate with.

Training and ending up with a loss or paying for training and earning profits? Well, it is entirely up to you to decide. What I can say is that having a mentor will prevent you from incurring unnecessary losses and result in a positive outcome.

Now that you are well equipped with the necessary information, it about time that you kick-start your journey in options trading. It is a good investment that can end with a favorable outcome. You know what it entails its pros and cons, the option strategies and tips for success, what else are you waiting for to start investing? You should be in the process of opening a brokerage account as you start your journey as an options trader. It is currently the 'coolest' investment to start trading. Life comes with endless opportunities, and options trading happens to be one of them. If you are looking for an investment that will completely transform your life, this is it. It is a convenient, reliable, and fantastic way to generate income. Some people have made it a full-time investment. This is because they have identified it as an investment that they can rely on for a successful outcome. If you are new to options trading, this is a perfect investment to carry out. The trick is to master the tactics that will increase your returns and minimize the risks. After all, the whole point of investing is to earn profits

There are a lot of different types of investments out there that you can choose to work with. Some are going to include taking over real estate and renting it out or selling it to others. Some will get into their own business and try to make money that way. And still, others will get into the stock market and hope they can make the right decisions.

But one investment that is different from all the others is options trading.

This guidebook has taken some time to talk about stock trading and all the neat things that you are able to do with it. We talked a bit about what stocks are and some of the benefits of choosing to work with them instead of with some of the other investments out there. In addition, this guidebook moved onto some of the best overall strategies that you can use with stock trading and what kind of market scenarios you encounter when using some of them.

As with any investment type, there is some risk involved when you get into stock trading. The good news is that we spent some time talking about the most common mistakes to avoid and how to reduce the amount of risk that you take on inside this investment opportunity. Stock investing is a tricky investment to choose to go with, but it provides a great return on investment and is often easier to get into compared to the stock market

It is a good idea to put all of this into a trading plan to summarize your approach to the markets. Think of it as your trading business plan for success. List your instruments to trade, which strategies you will follow, and how you will expand on them.

However, before proceeding you should master the material in this. The biggest problem for most traders is adjusting to the non-directional aspect of options. Understanding a stop loss and take profit is easy but dealing with a call option and a short put while experiencing a falling market tends to put their heads in a spin.

From novice to initiated, you have now gained the basics of knowledge that will help you enter the exciting world of stock trading. It certainly is not everything there is to know, but you now have enough of a grounding to get started.

From here out, it is all about practice and being conservative as you improve your understanding and develop your strategies. Only you will know what works best for you, how much risk you want to play with, and how your personal ability to predict and determine the stock market can be best put into practice.

As you dip your feet into the water, you will start to see profits coming in and you will feel that buzz all options traders enjoy. The more you trade, the more you will see all these fundamental mechanics at play, and the more you will start to connect the dots and figure out your personality as a trader.

You are in for a treat—stock trading is rewarding and exciting when done right. Remember to keep that calendar updated and to stay conservative at least in the beginning and you will enjoy that learning curves every step of the way!

Do not let one loss get you discouraged. The wealthiest traders and investors have all taken hits from which they thought they would never recover. Remember that you will have a few moments where you don't get as much back as you hoped but know that you will also have moments where you make more money than you ever did with your initial investment.

You have now had a careful stroll through the key standards and ventures in stock trading we feel are fundamental to progress as a stock trader. You have figured out how the stock markets function, the best trading strategies, and why it is basic to pick the best possible fundamental assets for the procedures you need to utilize.

You have additionally observed that great exit strategies are nearly as imperative as discovering great trades to enter, that focusing on the points of interest is basic, and that achievement is virtually inconceivable without a decent money-management plan—and the discipline to follow it.

At last, you have got lots of pages loaded with vital inquiries to consider in your search for the best online options broker. At the end of the day, it is a great opportunity to control up, plugin—and profit. You have all the data to appreciate 24-hour access to the options markets, fast and programmed execution of your orders, and the most reduced commissions in the history of options trading. In any case, to share these advantages, you should confront the lot bigger individual duties that accompany coordinate access to online trading.

You should have the discipline to do your very own research, screen your positions and monitor every one of the points of interest you may leave to your full-benefit financial firm. You can never again depend on a broker to watch your positions and call with guidance or suggestions. You are currently an autonomous administrator—and, all things considered, must be absolutely in charge of your behavior.

You should likewise be mindful and be prepared to react to both fast moves in everyday trading designs and consistently evolving longer-term economic situations.

Thank you for reading this all the way through to the end! I hope that you have found this to be informative and educational.

Stocks are a great way to get in the market with a lot less upfront capital. They can be tricky because they come with expiration dates, so you must get in and out at the right time and cannot wait things out like you can with a stock.

But the return on investment is far superior to stocks when you make profitable trades. Be sure to study the securities that you are investing in carefully so that you know where the stock has real potential to move.

Also, keep learning, and I hope this was a good start.

CPSIA information can be obtained
at www.ICGtesting.com
Printed in the USA
BVHW010752100821
613981BV00019B/88